BODY SYSTEMS

Blood and Circulation

Jackie Hardie

Heinemann

First published in Great Britain by Heinemann Library
Halley Court, Jordan Hill, Oxford OX2 8EJ
a division of Reed Educational and Professional Publishing Ltd

OXFORD FLORENCE PRAGUE MADRID ATHENS MELBOURNE
AUCKLAND KUALA LUMPUR SINGAPORE TOKYO IBADAN
NAIROBI KAMPALA JOHANNESBURG GABORONE
PORTSMOUTH NH (USA) CHICAGO MEXICO CITY SAO PAULO

Designed by Inklines and Small House Design
Illustrations by Oxford Illustrators, except: Peter Bull Art Studio, p.4 (left) &
pp 22-23; Garden Studio/Darren Patterson, p.27.

Printed in Great Britain by Bath Press Colourbooks, Glasgow
Originated in Great Britain by Dot Gradations, Wickford

01 00 99 98 97
10 9 8 7 6 5 4 3 2 1

ISBN 0 431 06211 0
This title is also available in a hardback library edition (ISBN 0 431 06210 2).

British Library Cataloguing in Publication Data
Hardie, Jackie, 1944 –
    Blood & circulation. – (Body systems)
    1. Blood – Juvenile literature 2. Circulation – Juvenile literature
    I. Title
    612.1

Acknowledgements
The Publishers would like to thank the following for permission to reproduce
photographs:
Corbis/Bettmann/UPI: p.26; The Mansell Collection: p.21; Oxford Scientific
Films: p.25 (bottom); Science Photo Library: p.5, p.6, p.7, p.9, p.11, p.13, p.17,
p.18, p.19, p.20, p.23, p.25 (top), p.29; Tony Stone Images: p.28 (right).

Cover photograph: Trevor Clifford.

Our thanks to Yvonne Hewson and Dr Kath Hadfield for their comments in
the preparation of this book.

Every effort has been made to contact copyright holders of any material
reproduced in this book. Any omissions will be rectified in subsequent printings
if notice is given to the Publisher.

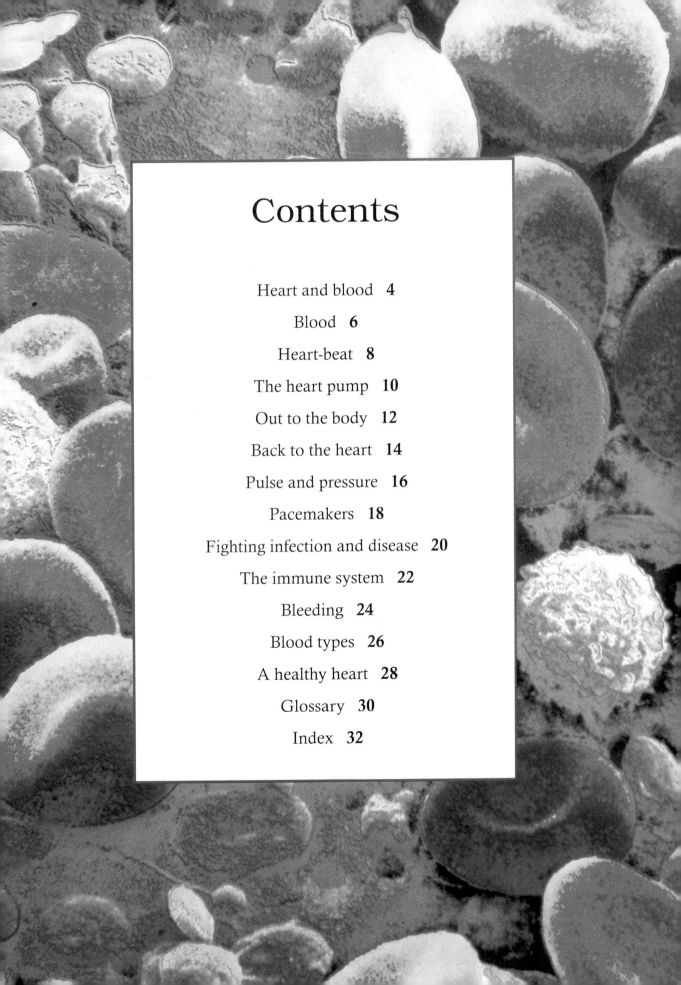

Contents

Heart and blood

Blood is the body's delivery and collection service. It delivers food and **oxygen** to every part of the body, and it collects waste products, particularly **carbon dioxide**. Blood circulates, or goes round and round your body, about 2000 times a day. It is pumped by the heart through tubes called blood vessels.

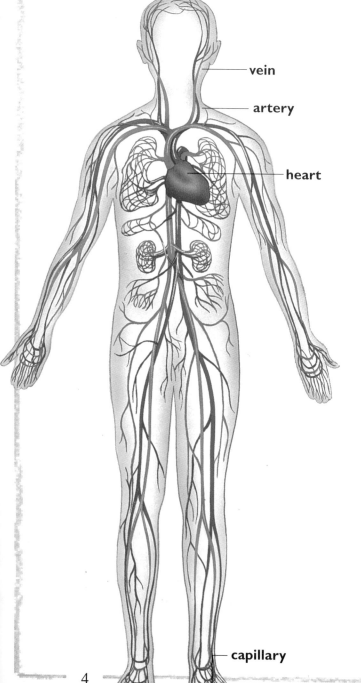

vein

artery

heart

capillary

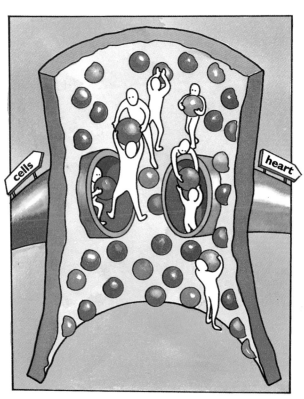

cells

heart

▲ Blood is a collection and delivery service for each **cell**. It brings food and oxygen, and collects waste.

◄ The heart pumps blood to every living cell. **Arteries** (shown in red) take it to different parts of the body, and **veins** (shown in blue) take it back to the heart.

Cells

Every part of your body is made up of millions of tiny cells, too small to see except through a microscope. Each kind of cell has a different job to do. All cells need oxygen, food and other chemicals to stay alive and do their job. Blood brings food and oxygen to each living cell in the body.

As each cell works, it uses oxygen to burn food to get energy, just as a car uses oxygen to burn fuel. In the process, the cell gives off carbon dioxide, like a car in its exhaust fumes. Blood carries this waste carbon dioxide away from each cell to the **lungs** where it is breathed out.

Moving things around

Blood travels away from your heart along blood vessels called arteries. Arteries branch into finer and finer tubes called **capillaries**, which spread out amongst the cells. Food and oxygen pass from the blood into the cells. The blood continues its journey through the capillaries to blood vessels called veins, which take it back to the heart. Blood travels only in one direction around the body, as in a one-way system.

▲ Every part of the body is made up of cells, even blood. Here, a smear of blood has been magnified about 500 times to show the different kinds of cells.

Did you know?

There are 80,000 km of blood vessels in your body. The biggest one is an artery which is 2.5 cm wide, and carries blood from the heart into the body. The smallest blood vessels are finer than a single hair. If all your blood vessels were laid out end-to-end, they would stretch twice around the world!

Blood

When you cut yourself, blood oozes out of the wound. Blood looks like thick red juice, but it is really a yellow liquid called **plasma** with different cells floating in it. Plasma is mainly water with **blood proteins** and food **molecules** dissolved in it. If you smear a drop of blood onto a thin layer of glass and then magnify it with a microscope, you can see the different cells in the plasma. There are **red cells**, **white cells** and **platelets**.

▲ Three types of blood cells viewed under a false-colour scanning electron micrograph microscope. You can see red blood cells, white blood cells, and, shown in blue, platelets.

Red cells

The most numerous kind of cell in your blood is the tiny saucer-shaped red blood cell. These cells are red because they contain a red substance called **haemoglobin**. Their main job is to carry oxygen from your **lungs** to other cells in the body. Oxygen is picked up and carried by the haemoglobin. Blood carrying oxygen, or **oxygenated blood**, is bright red. When the haemoglobin lets go of its oxygen, the colour changes to dull red.

Red blood cells live for only about 120 days. When they die they are broken up in the liver. New ones are made in the **red bone marrow**, which is found inside the main bones of the body. Some **capillaries** are so thin, the red cells have to change shape to squeeze along them.

White cells

There are several types of white cell, and they can live for a long time – some as long as 40 years! White blood cells are made by bone marrow too, and help to defend the body against disease.

Platelets

Platelets are very tiny cells with a sticky surface and no **nucleus**. They help to seal wounds, and are also made by bone marrow.

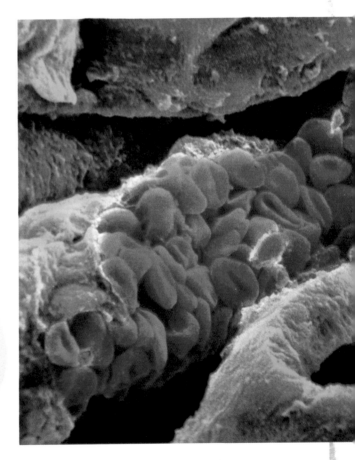

▲ Red cells can change their shape because the **membrane** which covers them is stretchy.

Did you know?

A tiny drop of blood about the size of a pin head contains 5 million red cells, 7000 white cells and 250,000 platelets. An adult body holds about 5 litres of blood, so that means that there are around 15 billion red cells in it!

Heart-beat

Your heart pumps blood around your body. If you put your hand in the middle of your chest, just over the chest bone, you will feel it beating. It is made of very strong muscle, called cardiac muscle, which never gets tired. This keeps your heart beating day and night, every day of your life. The heart is held in place beneath the ribs and between the **lungs** by strong threads. It looks nothing like the pictures on Valentine cards! An adult's heart is as big as their clenched fist. Yours is smaller – about the size of your own fist.

Inside the heart

When a heart is cut open, you can see a thick wall down the middle, dividing it up into two halves – a left and a right side. The heart is really two pumps working side by side. Each pump has a top space, or **atrium**, which receives blood from the veins. Below each atrium is another space, a **ventricle**, which pumps blood out of the heart and into arteries.

▶ *What the heart looks like inside. The muscle squeezes the blood in each chamber through the narrow valve. This gives the blood enough 'push' to get to all the main parts of the body.*

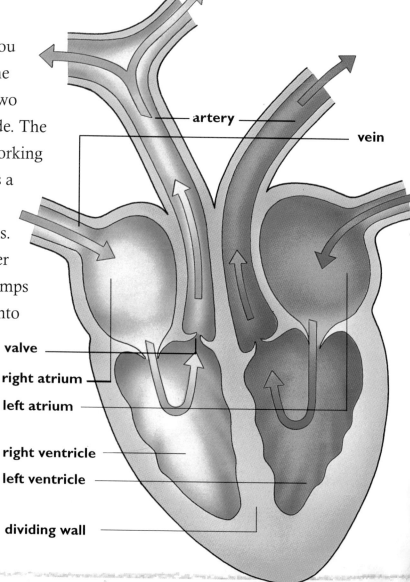

artery

vein

valve

right atrium

left atrium

right ventricle

left ventricle

dividing wall

A regular beat

An adult heart beats between 60 and 70 times every minute. That is about 4000 times in one hour and nearly 100,000 times every day. During an average life, a heart will beat about 2500 million times. Children's hearts beat faster than adults' hearts.

If you start to move about or take any kind of exercise, your heart beats faster. This is because during exercise your body **cells** need more **oxygen.** Your heart must work harder to get blood carrying oxygen to your cells quickly.

Supplying the heart

Your heart does not take food and oxygen from the blood passing through it. Your heart has its own blood supply – the **coronary blood vessels**. The coronary arteries supply heart muscle with oxygen and food. Waste is taken away by coronary veins.

◄ *A real heart does not look very romantic. It is a very powerful muscle, weighing about 300 grams in adults.*

Did you know?

Animals' hearts beat at different rates than ours. Surprisingly, the bigger the animal, the slower the heart beat. An elephant's heart beats 27 times every minute, whilst in the same time, the heart of a canary beats an amazing 1000 times!

The heart pump

Your heart is made of two strong muscular pumps which work together to push blood around the body in a continuous cycle. The right side pumps blood to the **lungs** to pick up **oxygen**, and the left side pumps this **oxygenated blood** to the rest of the body. Used or **de-oxygenated blood** travels back to the heart through the **veins**, and the cycle begins again.

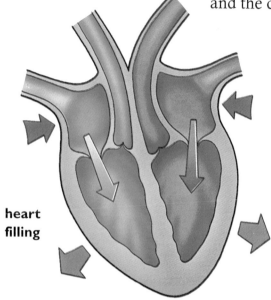

heart filling

▲ The valves between the atria and the ventricles open to allow blood to flow into the ventricles.

Filling and emptying the heart

Blood is returned to the heart into the **atria**. When the **muscle fibres** in the **ventricles** relax, the space inside the ventricles gets bigger. Blood is sucked in from the atria to fill the ventricles. When the muscle fibres in the ventricles **contract**, the ventricle walls press on the blood inside, forcing it out into the **arteries**.

Blood is always pushed out of the heart in the right direction, because there are tough **heart valves** between the atria and ventricles which stop blood flowing back the wrong way.

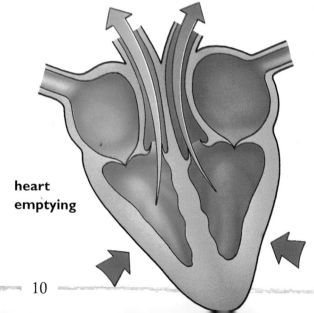

heart emptying

◄ As the ventricles contract, the valves to the atria close, so blood goes out into the arteries.

Valves

Heart valves snap open and closed. When they snap open, they let blood go through the heart in one direction only, from the atrium into the ventricle. As the ventricles contract to push blood out into the arteries, the valves slam shut, so the blood cannot flow back into the two atria.

Other valves are found inside the openings of the arteries. These valves look like half-moons, so they are called semi-lunar valves. Like the heart valves, the semi-lunar valves let the blood move one way only, from ventricle to artery.

Heart sounds

If you listen to someone's heart beat, you can hear a 'lub-dup' sound. The 'lub' sound is made by the heart valves slamming shut. The 'dup' sound is made when the semi-lunar valves close.

Did you know?

If a person's heart valves do not shut properly, he or she may get a heart murmur. Sometimes a faulty valve can be replaced by an artificial one. Today, scientists are trying to grow human cells to make replacement valves.

Out to the body

Your heart, blood vessels and blood work together to move **cells** and chemicals around your body in one-way routes. The main **artery**, or **aorta**, leaves the left side of your heart. It is over 2.5 cm wide, and branches many times to form important arteries. Each one goes to a different part of the body. The **pulmonary artery** leaves the right side of the heart. It divides into two, so one artery can go to each **lung**. Blood in these arteries picks up **oxygen** in the lungs, then returns to the left side of the heart, to be sent around the body. So the blood carried in the aorta and its branches is **oxygenated**.

Types of blood vessels

Arteries carry blood away from the heart, and **veins** bring blood back to the heart. How does the blood get from the arteries to the veins? These two types of blood vessel are connected by fine branching networks of **capillaries**. Capillaries are very narrow tubes which pass close to every living cell in your body. The walls of the capillaries are extremely thin, so chemicals can easily enter or leave the blood through them.

► *Arteries and veins are linked by networks of capillaries.*

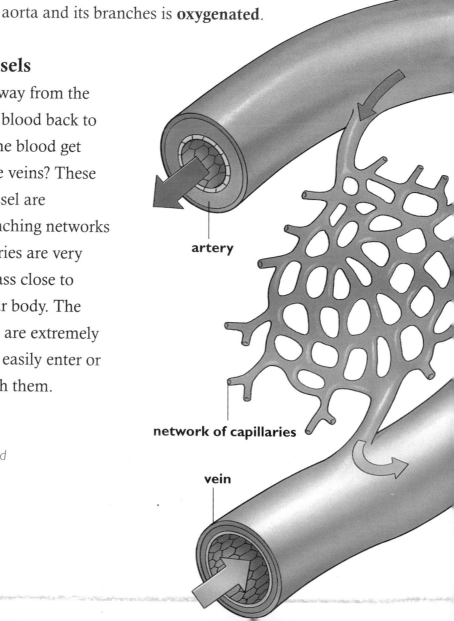

artery

network of capillaries

vein

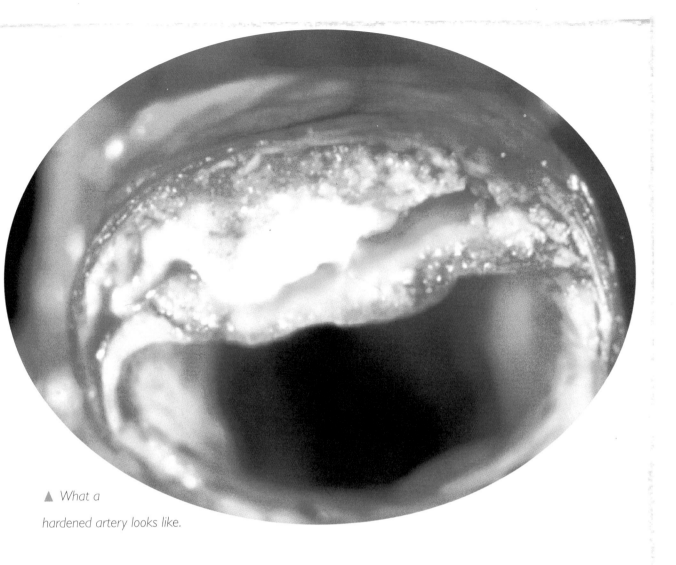

▲ *What a*

hardened artery looks like.

Hardened arteries

Some people's arteries become harder and thicker as they get older. This means the heart has to work more to pump blood through them. The hardening takes place in two stages. First a fatty substance sticks to the arteries' inside lining.

Then the fibres in the walls become thicker and harder. What causes this is not known for sure, but doctors agree that a healthy diet, not smoking, regular exercise and relaxation, and not being overweight all help to avoid it.

Did you know?

Water is what makes your blood runny so it can flow around your body. More than half your blood is plasma, and nine-tenths of plasma is water.

Back to the heart

Blood travels back to the heart along **veins**. Two large veins called the **venae cavae** pour blood into the right **atrium**. The **pulmonary veins** return blood to the left atrium. When blood surges through your **arteries**, their walls stretch and then spring back, giving the blood an extra push. The walls of your veins are not as thick and stretchy. Instead, valves help to move blood along.

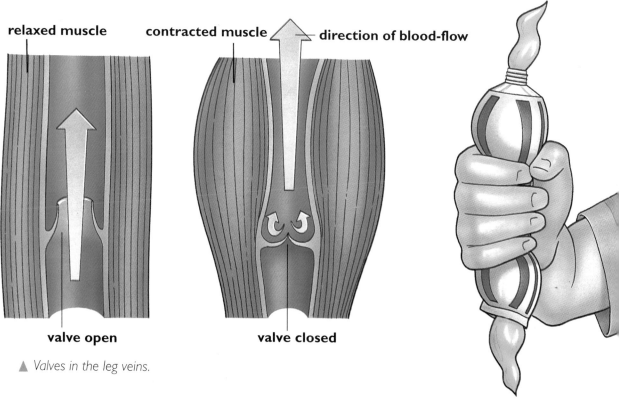

relaxed muscle   contracted muscle   direction of blood-flow

valve open   valve closed

▲ *Valves in the leg veins.*

Vein valves

The veins in your legs and arms thread their way between muscle. As the muscles work, they squeeze the veins and push the blood along. Valves stop the blood moving in the wrong way. What would happen if the valves were not there?

Imagine squeezing a tube of toothpaste with the cap off and the end split. When you squeezed the tube, the toothpaste would squirt out at both ends. The valves' job is to stop this happening to the blood in your veins.

Varicose veins

Older people may get varicose veins when the valves in their veins no longer work properly. This condition can be quite painful, and gives a lumpy appearance to the back of the legs. You can avoid getting varicose veins by doing plenty of exercise. This helps to return the blood to the heart.

Hole in the heart

Some babies are born with a gap or hole in their heart between the left and right atrium. This means that **oxygenated** and **de-oxygenated blood** mix together, and some blood may not go to the **lungs** at all. Surgeons close the hole by cutting open the heart and putting plastic netting over it. A scar forms over the net and seals the hole.

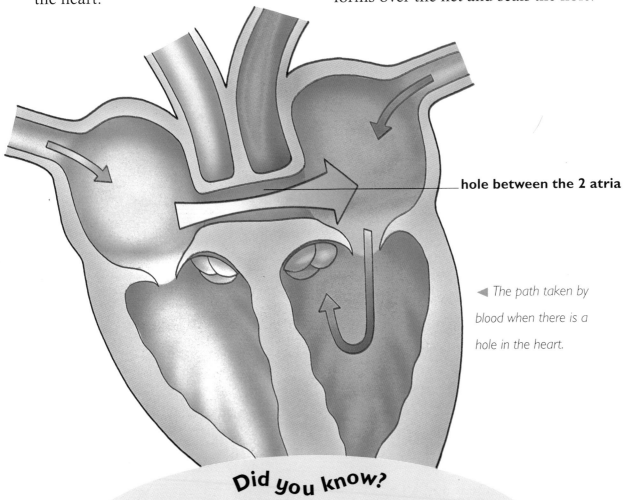

hole between the 2 atria

◄ The path taken by blood when there is a hole in the heart.

Did you know?

A light-skinned baby born with a hole in the heart looks blue. In 1944 the first open-heart surgery was performed on a 'blue baby'. The baby had only a narrow artery connecting the heart to the lungs. The surgeon inserted an artificial tube between the heart and the lungs.

Pulse and pressure

If someone has a bad accident and cuts an **artery**, bright red blood will gush out in spurts. Each spurt happens when the **ventricles** of the heart contract. As blood is pushed into an artery, its wall stretches. As the heart relaxes, the wall springs back. This movement of the artery walls allows doctors to measure both your **pulse rate** and your **blood pressure**.

Feeling your pulse

You can feel blood spurting through an artery at a pressure point. Here, the artery lies close to the surface of the skin, and can be pressed against a bone. You can take your own pulse by putting your fingers on the inside of your other wrist. Press your fingertips gently on the pulse, and count the number of beats or pulses in one minute. This is your pulse rate. Doctors count your pulse rate to tell if your heart is working normally.

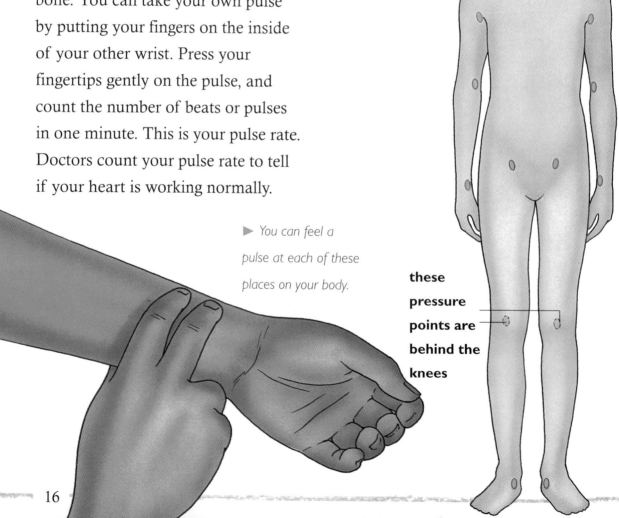

▶ *You can feel a pulse at each of these places on your body.*

these pressure points are behind the knees

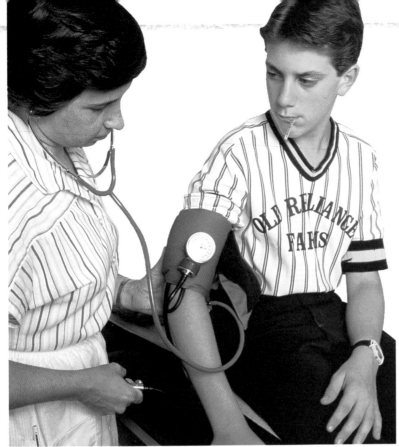

◀ A doctor takes a patient's blood pressure. It tells her if the elastic walls of the arteries are healthy.

Measuring blood pressure

The walls of your arteries are elastic. When blood is pumped into them, they are pushed outwards. This push is the blood pressure. A doctor first measures the pressure when the ventricles contract to push blood into the arteries.

Then the pressure is measured a second time when the heart is refilling. So, blood pressure is given as two numbers – one for each measurement. A healthy adult's blood pressure is around 120/80, although this will vary slightly from person to person.

Did you know?

When you are frightened or angry, happy or excited, your heart beats faster. You may even feel it pounding away in your chest. Your blood pressure and pulse rate increase, too. Because changes in your emotions cause your heart to change, people used to think that our feelings came from our heart. That is how phrases such as 'My heart was in my mouth', 'He's warm-hearted' and 'I'm heartbroken' began.

Pacemakers

Your heart muscle's natural beat is controlled by a group of **cells** called the **pacemaker**, found in the right **atrium**. The pacemaker produces a small wave of electricity which spreads through the heart muscle and makes the fibres **contract**. This electrical wave can be picked up by machines and recorded.

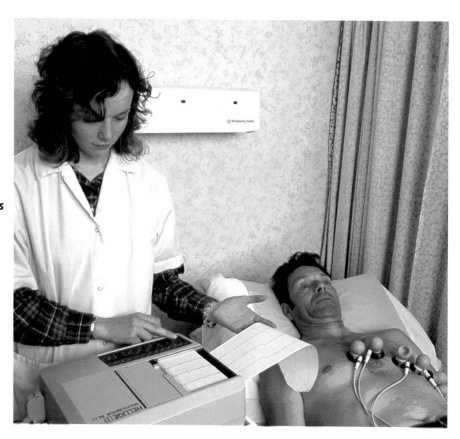

► *This patient is fitted with* **electrodes** *which pick up the activity of his heart's pacemaker.*

The heart's pacemaker

The heart's pacemaker can be checked by placing electrodes on the skin in different places around the chest. The electrical messages picked up by the electrodes can be displayed on a screen or they can be printed out and studied.

The device which converts the electrical wave in the heart to a display is an electrocardiograph (ECG). The printout is an ECG trace. By studying the trace, doctors can spot if there is anything wrong with someone's natural pacemaker.

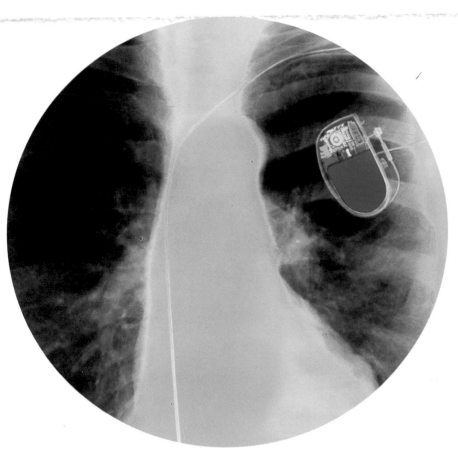

◄ This X-ray of a human chest shows an artificial heart pacemaker in position. The wire carries electricity to the walls of the **ventricles** to make their muscle fibres contract.

Artificial pacemakers

If the heart's pacemaker is faulty, the heart can be helped with an artificial pacemaker. The first devices were so large, they were placed on a trolley near the patient, who was then connected to it. Today's pacemakers are smaller than a matchbox, thanks to **micro-electronics**, and are powered by lithium batteries.

A pacemaker is fixed beneath the skin to the left of the patient's heart, where the doctor can get at it easily to change the batteries when they need it, every 5 to 12 years. A wire goes from the battery to the wall of the ventricle. This wire supplies a wave of electricity to make the ventricles contract.

Did you know?

Detectors at the security area in an airport can pick up if someone is carrying metal. When travellers walk through the security arch, a signal sounds if they are carrying any metal. Keys and coins set the alarm off, and so do pacemakers! People fitted with a pacemaker are warned not to pass through these metal detectors.

Fighting infection and disease

Your body is continually under attack from microbes – **bacteria**, **viruses** and **fungi** – that may cause disease. To help you stay healthy and avoid infection, your body has ways of keeping these microbes out, and dealing with them if they do get in! The skin, breathing tubes and stomach are your body's first line of defence. If they fail, your blood is in reserve.

First line of defence

Your skin is a barrier. If it is intact, it keeps out the microbes. Some parts of your body, like your eyes, nose and mouth are not protected by skin. Here, the fluids, tears and **saliva** can destroy bacteria. Your nose and throat, however, are direct routes into your body. Microbes may be trapped in the breathing tubes by the sticky mucus which lines the walls. Tiny hairs move this mucus towards the throat and you swallow it. You also swallow microbes in the food you eat, but the **cells** in the stomach make acid which can kill most 'invaders'.

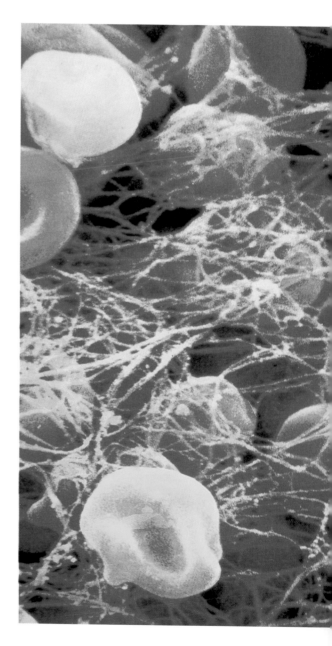

▶ **Red blood cells**

covered in fibrin – a sticky substance which helps form a scab.

Reserve defence – the blood

When skin is cut or grazed, it opens up a direct route into the body. In itself a small cut is not dangerous, but it can allow microbes to get in. Bleeding helps to wash out many of these microbes. **White blood cells** attack the rest.

▼ *The most famous haemophiliac, Alexis, son of the last Russian tsar. Today, haemophiliacs are given* **transfusions** *of factor VIII, but there was no such treatment in his time.*

If a blood vessel is damaged, it is sealed by a blood clot to stop too much blood being lost. The plug stops infection, too. At the wound, **platelets** stick to the damaged cells and send out chemical messengers which trigger off a chain of changes. A sticky net of **fibrin threads** forms over the wound. This soon gets plugged with red blood cells, which dry and form a scab. New skin grows under the scab to seal the wound. Then the scab drops off. Shiny new skin is revealed beneath it.

Haemophilia

The substances in the blood which make it clot are given Roman numerals (I to XII). **Haemophiliacs** have no factor VIII, so their blood takes a long time to clot. Any wound bleeds a lot and for a long time. Just the movement of their joints can sometimes cause bleeding and bruising.

Did you know?

Haemophilia *is a disease passed on from parents to children. Alexis, the son of the last Russian tsar, suffered from haemophilia. Both parents had normal blood, but his mother carried the disease and gave it to her son.*

21

The immune system

If microbes overcome the body's first line of defence and get into your body, they are much more difficult to deal with. They multiply quickly, and may even attack your body **cells** or release poisons called toxins into the blood. This can damage your body, and may bring about disease. Your body has to identify the dangerous microbes and destroy them without damaging its own cells. This is the job of the **immune system**, and the different **white blood cells** are the most important part of it.

The body's fighting force

Some white cells destroy microbes by surrounding them. But if these white cells are overcome by the invading microbes, there is yet another line of defence. Other kinds of white blood cells recognize a particular type of microbe, and respond by producing a defence chemical called an **antibody**. This antibody fits around the microbe, just like a glove, and stops it from doing any more harm. If this particular microbe has tried to invade your body before, the reaction is even faster because the antibody has already been made. Each kind of antibody only works against one particular kind of microbe.

▶ *This cell recognizes the microbe as an invader. It surrounds the microbe and kills it.*

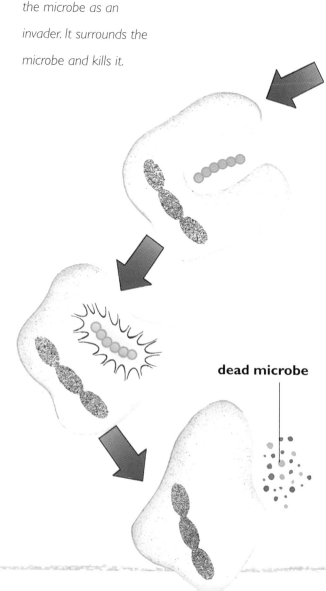

dead microbe

► The boy behind the plastic wall was born with a faulty immune system. He has no natural defence against infection by microbes. The plastic bubble protects him.

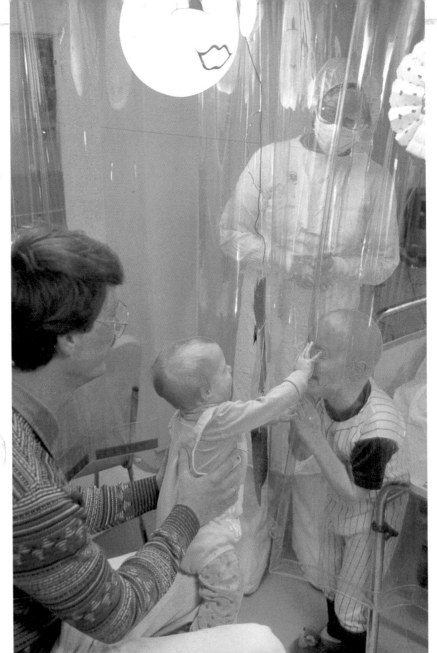

microbe

Did you know?

In the early 1980s, doctors noticed more and more patients with faulty immune systems. They were suffering from a wide range of very unusual infections. These patients had not been born with the condition. They had never had complicated surgery either. These new cases were described as having 'acquired immune deficiency syndrome', a long name which has now been shortened to AIDS.

Bleeding

Knowing what to do when you have a cut or wound can make all the difference to how quickly it heals. It is just as important to know how to react if there is a serious accident and people near you are badly injured.

Minor cuts

You should wash a small cut in clean, cold water. If the wound is dirty, then dab it with clean cotton wool which has been dipped in a mild antiseptic such as iodine. The bleeding normally stops quickly. If it doesn't, press a clean dressing, such as a plaster or cotton wool, tightly over the wound for a few minutes.

Nose bleeds

The lining of your nasal passages has lots of very fine blood vessels. Sometimes they may burst and cause a nose bleed, but this bleeding will stop quickly if correctly treated. If you have a nose bleed, lean forward over a sink or bowl to catch the blood and pinch the nose just beneath the bony bit. A heavy nose bleed may make you feel faint. If so, you must rest for a short time.

Serious bleeding

Losing lots of blood can be very dangerous. It is important to get trained help very quickly. In the UK you can summon help by dialling 999 on the telephone. While you are waiting, get someone to help the patient by padding the wound and raising the injured part. It is best if everyone keeps calm.

◄ *The correct position for treating a nose bleed.*

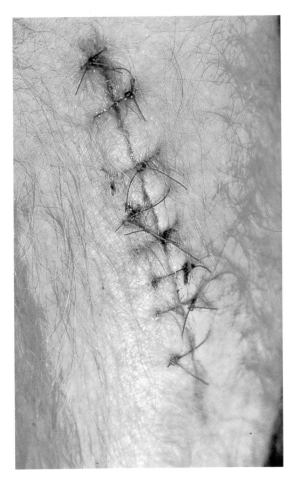

◄ *These stitches hold together the sides of a wound, so that the opening into the body is sealed.*

▼ *Today, doctors act quickly to stop bleeding. In the past they thought that removing blood, or bleeding, a patient was a good thing. They used leeches to suck blood from their patients. Even today, doctors may use leeches to remove blood from bruises near badly injured eyes.*

At the hospital, a doctor or nurse will hold the sides of the wound together to help seal it. If the wound is large, they may use stitches to hold the sides together. Anyone with a serious cut should never be given anything to eat or drink, because they may need an anaesthetic. This is a drug which will make them unconscious during an operation. If the patient has had something to eat or drink beforehand, they may choke or vomit during the operation.

Did you know?

Until the nineteenth century, doctors regularly used to use leeches to 'bleed' patients. The patients did not feel anything because leeches' saliva contains an anaesthetic that numbs the skin.

Blood types

If a person is badly injured or has major surgery, they may lose a lot of blood. One-sixth of all the blood in the body can be lost without serious damage. If more is lost, the body will stop working properly. Blood is made inside the body to replace any that is lost, but this takes time. Blood can be taken from a healthy person (a donor) and given to someone who needs it (a recipient) in a blood **transfusion**. The right kind of blood must be given for this to work.

The discovery of blood groups

At the end of the nineteenth century, when people were given blood transfusions, the patients sometimes survived and sometimes didn't. When the transfusions did not work, doctors noticed that the **red blood cells** were sticking together. The clumps they made clogged up the **capillaries** and stopped blood flowing through them.

An Austrian, Karl Landsteiner, wanted to find out why the red cells sometimes went sticky. He knew that blood always looked the same under a microscope, but he set out to prove that everybody's blood is not the same. He discovered the types of blood we know as the ABO groups.

▲ Karl Landsteiner first reported his findings on blood types in 1900. But it was not until 1908 that the first transfusion under safe conditions was carried out by Reuben Ottenburg in New York.

Landsteiner's work

Landsteiner took blood samples from different people. He separated each sample into the **plasma** and red cell parts, then mixed the individual plasmas with different samples of red cells. Sometimes the cells stuck together, and sometimes not. He realized there was a reaction between some plasmas and some red cells.

When there was a match between the chemicals in the plasma and in the red cells, the cells did not become sticky. When there was a mismatch, the cells clumped together. This is how he discovered four types of human blood – A, B, AB and O – each with a different type of **blood protein** on its red cells' **membranes**.

Blood groups around the world

The number of people with a particular blood group varies from one part of the world to another. About 46 per cent of people in the world have blood group O. This is the most common blood group. In Norway, though, the most common group is A. The rarest group worldwide is AB. In the British Isles less than three per cent of the population have this group.

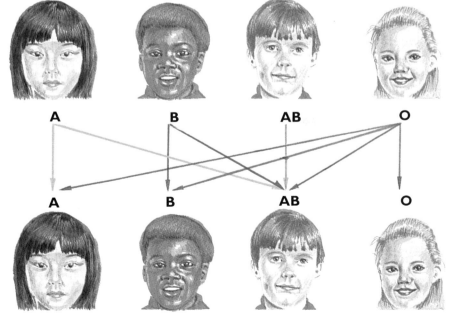

A   B   AB   O

A   B   AB   O

◄ *People with blood group O can give blood to all groups, but receive from group O only. Group AB can receive from all groups, but give only to AB.*

A healthy heart

Heart disease is the single biggest killer in the UK. Many of these deaths could be avoided, if we changed our unhealthy life style. If you get into practice now, you are likely to cut down the risk of getting heart disease when you are older.

Exercise

Like any other muscle, the heart will become stronger if extra demands are put on it by regular and vigorous exercise. When you exercise, your body muscles need more **oxygen**, so the heart has to pump faster to increase the supply. However, a fit heart does not have to work as hard, or beat as fast, as an unfit heart.

This is because it pumps more blood with each beat. Exercise also keeps your **blood pressure** low, as it helps your **arteries** keep their elasticity. To get fit, take part at least once a week in exercise which increases your heart rate for 20 to 30 minutes.

▲ *Athletes are fit and have bigger hearts than most people because they develop the muscles of their heart with regular exercise.*

◄ *Being active helps to keep your heart healthy.*

Diet

The heart of an overweight person has to strain to supply blood for the extra weight in the body. If you eat too much animal fat, some may stick to the walls of your arteries. These narrow and 'fur up' like blocked pipes. Some bits of fat may fall off and form a clot, which can block the flow of blood. If a clot blocks a **capillary** in the brain it causes a **stroke**. A clot in the heart itself causes a **heart attack**.

Smoking

Nicotine, the drug in tobacco, causes the **muscle fibres** in the walls of arteries to **contract**. It narrows the channel through which blood flows. If this takes place in the arteries supplying the heart, the amount of blood carrying oxygen and food to the heart is reduced. If the artery walls have lost some of their elasticity, or have fatty deposits on them too, then nicotine may block the blood vessel, causing a heart attack.

Stress

When you are excited your heart beats faster. This is not bad for the heart if you have time to calm down afterwards. But if you stay angry, stressed or worried for a long time, then your heart-beat will stay high, which strains it.

▲ The Jarvik 7 was powered by compressed air.

Did you know?

To help people with diseased hearts, doctors have made artificial hearts. These were invented by an American, Robert Jarvik. The first one, known as the Jarvik 7, was implanted in 1982, but the patient only survived for 112 days. Doctors prefer to use heart transplants rather than artificial hearts, because they are more reliable. One day, doctors may use pigs' hearts for transplants.

Glossary

Antibody A defence chemical given off by certain white blood cells in response to the invasion of the body by microbes. The antibody stops the invading microbe and stops it from doing any more harm. Each kind of antibody works against one particular type of microbe.

Aorta The largest artery in the body, which leaves the left side of the heart.

Artery A type of blood vessel which carries blood away from the heart, around the body.

Atrium The name given to the upper part, or chamber, of the heart which receives blood from the veins. The heart has two atria, one on the left side and one on the right side.

Bacteria Single living cells that function independently. They are so small that we can only see them through a microscope. There are millions of bacteria in the air around us and in our bodies. Most are harmless, but some can cause diseases.

Blood pressure The push of the blood against the elastic walls of the arteries. Doctors measure blood pressure as the heart contracts and blood surges through the arteries, pushing the walls outwards. They also measure it when the heart relaxes, and the walls spring back into place. Blood pressure is expressed as two numbers; 120/80 is a normal blood pressure for a healthy adult.

Blood proteins Substances found in plasma. They are also on the walls of red blood cells and determine the person's blood group.

Capillaries Very thin blood vessels – blood cells squeeze through them in single file.

Carbon dioxide The waste gas given off by cells when they use oxygen to burn food to release energy. Blood collects this waste gas from the cells and carries it to the lungs where it is breathed out.

Cells The smallest living unit. Each part of the body is built up of a different kind of cell. Most cells have a nucleus which controls what the cell does, and each cell is surrounded by a membrane.

Contract To become shorter and thicker. When muscle contracts, the muscle fibres slide alongside each other, and this makes the muscle block shorter .

Coronary blood vessels The blood vessels which keep the heart muscle supplied with food and oxygen, and take away waste products.

De-oxygenated blood Blood which has already visited cells and given up its oxygen to them. De-oxygenated blood is a dull red colour.

Electrodes Devices which are used to conduct an electrical current.

Fibrin threads Sticky threads which form over a wound to trap red blood cells. The red blood cells dry out in this mesh to form a scab.

Fungi Simple living things which live on dead or living things, or on food.

Haemophilia A disease which is passed on from parents to children. Sufferers' blood contains no factor VIII, an essential clotting agent, so their blood takes a very long time to clot when they cut or wound themselves. Even a very slight cut can bleed a lot.

Haemophiliac The name given to someone who suffers from haemophilia.

Haemoglobin The red substance found in red blood cells which gives them their colour. It is the haemoglobin which picks up oxygen in the lungs, carries it around the body in the blood, and finally delivers it to cells.

Heart attack If one of the blood vessels supplying the heart with oxygen and food becomes blocked, the heart cannot work properly. This is known as a heart attack.

Heart murmur A medical condition caused by faulty heart valves. The valves do not shut properly.

Heart valves Tough flaps, found between the atria and the ventricles of the heart, which stop blood flowing in the wrong direction. They snap open to let blood flow from the atria into the ventricles, and then slam shut as the ventricles contract to push blood out of the heart into the arteries.

Immune system The system which defends the body against harmful microbes. It identifies 'foreign invaders', and destroys them without damaging the body's own cells.

Lungs Two organs within the chest cavity which are used to breathe. When air is breathed into the lungs, the blood there absorbs oxygen from the air, and releases carbon dioxide to be breathed out.

Membrane A thin layer which surrounds different parts of the body, for example single cells or blocks of muscle.

Micro-electronics The design, making and use of electronic equipment using extremely small parts, in particular silicon chips.

Molecules The smallest possible parts of a substance capable of existing independently.

Muscle fibres Thin strands of muscle which are gathered together in bundles. Together, these bundles form muscle tissue.

Nucleus A cell's control centre, which tells it what to do.

Oxygen A gas which is needed by every living cell in the body to live and work. It is found in the air we breathe, along with several other gases.

Oxygenated blood Blood which is carrying oxygen to the cells of the body. It is bright red.

Pacemaker A group of cells found in the heart which gives off an electrical wave, causing the heart muscle to contract regularly. The pacemaker controls the beating of the heart.

Plasma A yellow liquid which forms the basis of blood. It is made of water, with food molecules, blood proteins and other chemicals dissolved in it.

Platelet A kind of blood cell with no nucleus which helps to seal wounds.

Pulmonary artery The main artery leaving the right side of the heart. It divides into two, so that one artery can go to each lung.

Pulmonary veins These veins return oxygenated blood to the left atrium of the heart.

Pulse rate The number of times your heart beats, measured as the number of times your heart beats in one minute. Your pulse rate goes up when you exercise, and when you are angry or excited. Your pulse rate is slower when you relax.

Red bone marrow A soft, red, jelly-like substance which is found at the centre of some bones. It makes white and red blood cells.

Red (blood) cells One kind of cell found in the blood which contains a red oxygen-carrying substance called haemoglobin. Their job is to transport oxygen around the body in the blood.

Saliva The liquid made by the salivary glands in the mouth. It is produced when you see, smell, think about or chew food. It helps food to slip down your throat more easily, and contains chemicals which start to digest the food.

Stroke If a blockage occurs in a capillary which supplies the brain with oxygen and food, the brain cannot work properly. This is known as a stroke.

Transfusion When blood is taken from a healthy person and given to someone who needs it, usually during an operation or after an accident, if the patient has lost a lot of blood.

Veins Blood vessels which carry de-oxygenated blood.

Venae cavae The two large veins which pour blood back into the right atrium.

Ventricle The name given to the lower part, or chamber of the heart. It has a strong muscular wall to push blood out into the arteries and around the body. The heart has two ventricles, one on the right side and one on the left side.

Virus A disease-producing microbe which can only be seen using an electron microscope.

White (blood) cells One kind of cell found in the blood. There are several types of white blood cell, but they are all part of the immune system, and are used to fight infection in the body.

Index

Your Body

Eating

Anna Sandeman

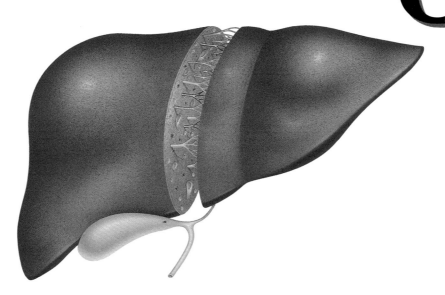

W
FRANKLIN WATTS
LONDON • SYDNEY

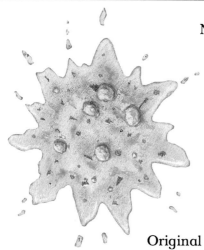

New edition published in 2002
© Aladdin Books Ltd 2002
Designed and produced by
Aladdin Books Ltd
28 Percy Street
London W1T 2BZ

First published in
Great Britain in 2002 by
Franklin Watts
96 Leonard Street
London EC2A 4XD

Original edition published by
Franklin Watts in 1995

Design: David West Children's Book Design
Designer: Edward Simkins
Illustrator: Ian Thompson
Editor: Liz White
Picture Research: Brooks Krikler
Research
Consultants: Dr R Levene MB.BS,
DCH, DRCOG
Jan Bastoncino Dip. Ed., teacher of
biology and science to 5-12 year-olds

ISBN 0-7496-4827-9

Photocredits: Abbreviations: t-top, m-middle, b-
bottom, r-right, l-left
All the photos in this book are by Roger Vlitos
except: 6t, 7t, 8-9b, 13b, 23tr, 23mr & 28-29t
Frank Spooner Pictures; 22r & 23br Paul
Nightingale; 23l Eye Ubiquitous; 28m Associated
British Pictures Co. (Courtesy Kobal Collection.)

Contents

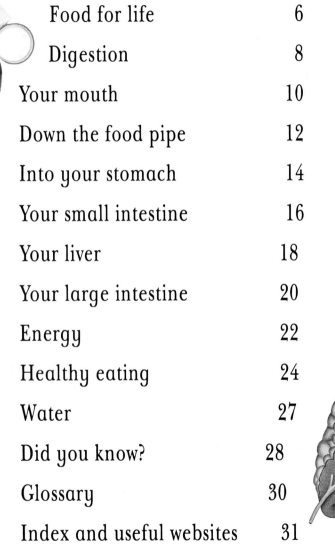

Food for life

All animals must eat to stay alive. Food is needed for energy and for growth. Food also helps to mend parts of the body which have been hurt, or have gone wrong.

The kind of food each animal eats depends on where it lives, its size, shape and strength. Monkeys will eat almost anything they can find. Penguins dive for fish in the icy Antarctic sea. They swallow a fish in a single gulp. Lions chase zebra across the hot African plains.

People live all over the world. They eat a wide variety of foods, prepared and cooked in many different ways. They can eat with their fingers, with chopsticks, or with forks, knives and spoons. But whatever people eat, and however they eat it, food is of no use to the body until it has been digested.

Digestion

Digestion starts as soon as you put food in your mouth. It carries on for about 18 hours as the food travels through your digestive system. This is a series of tunnels and caves inside your body. These are all different sizes, shapes and lengths.

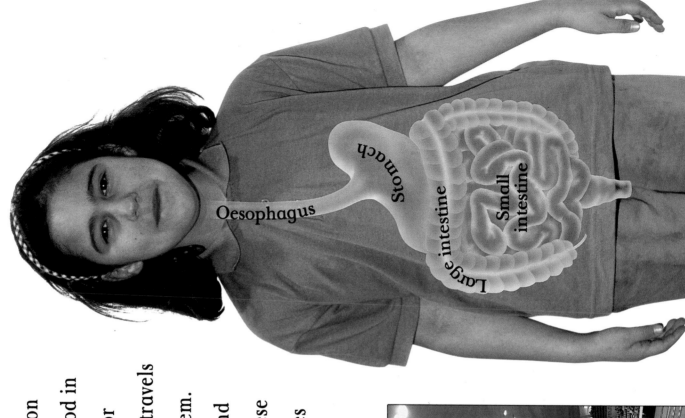

Oesophagus

Stomach

Large intestine

Small intestine

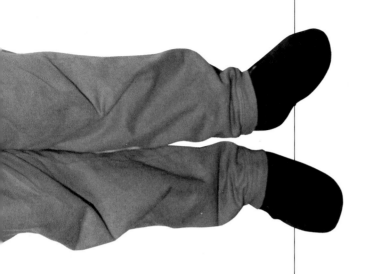

If they were laid in a straight line, they would stretch over eight metres – the width of an average swimming pool!

Your body digests food slowly by breaking it down into smaller and smaller pieces, separating it into useful parts – nutrients and waste matter. Food is completely digested when it has passed from your digestive system into your blood. Your blood then carries the nutrients around your body.

Food is broken down in the digestive system.

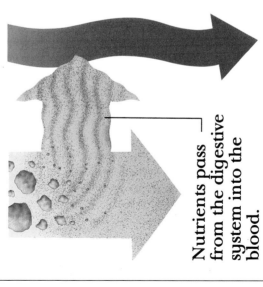

Nutrients pass from the digestive system into the blood.

Your mouth

Each part of your mouth has a special job to do. If you eat an apple, you bite into it with your front teeth. The four teeth in the middle of your top and bottom jaws, your incisors, are used for cutting and chopping. The sharp, fang-like teeth either side of your incisors are used for cutting and tearing. These are your canine teeth.

Your tongue pushes the apple back to your molars for chewing.

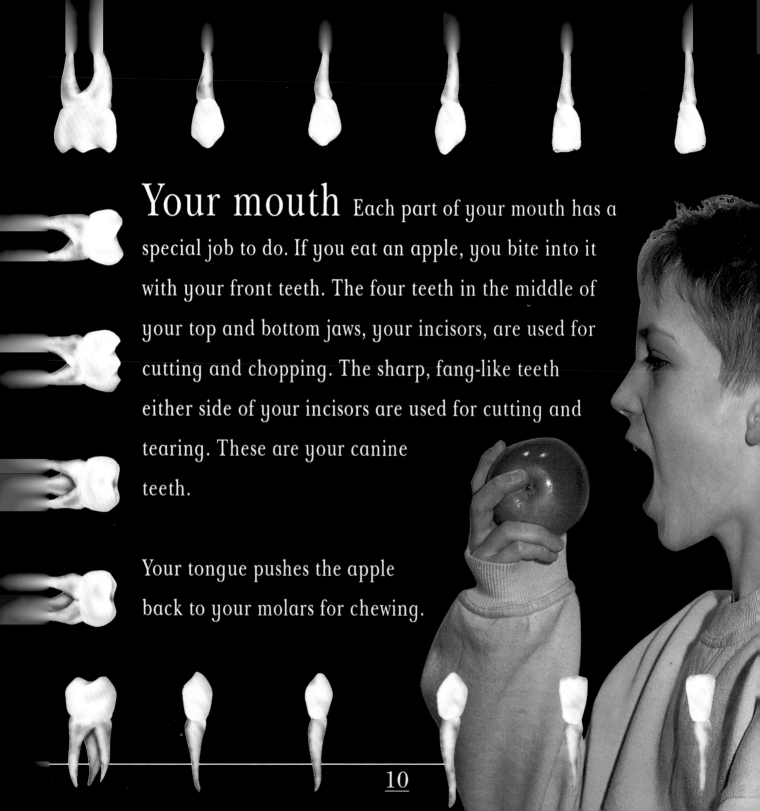

Incisor   Canine   Molar

You have molars in both your upper and lower jaws. Your molars are wider than your front teeth and have bumpy tops. Run a finger along the edges of your upper teeth and feel the difference.

Your molars grind the apple until it becomes a lumpy mash. Your tongue rolls the mash into a ball.

Saliva in your mouth makes chewing easier, it also helps you to taste. Sometimes just thinking about your favourite food will make your mouth fill with saliva. Try it and see.

Down the food pipe

Your tongue pushes the ball of mash into your food pipe. This is called your oesophagus. As you swallow, a flap (your epiglottis) drops over your windpipe. This stops food going down the wrong way.

Sometimes your epiglottis does not drop down in time. When this happens, you have to cough hard until the food is blown out of your windpipe.

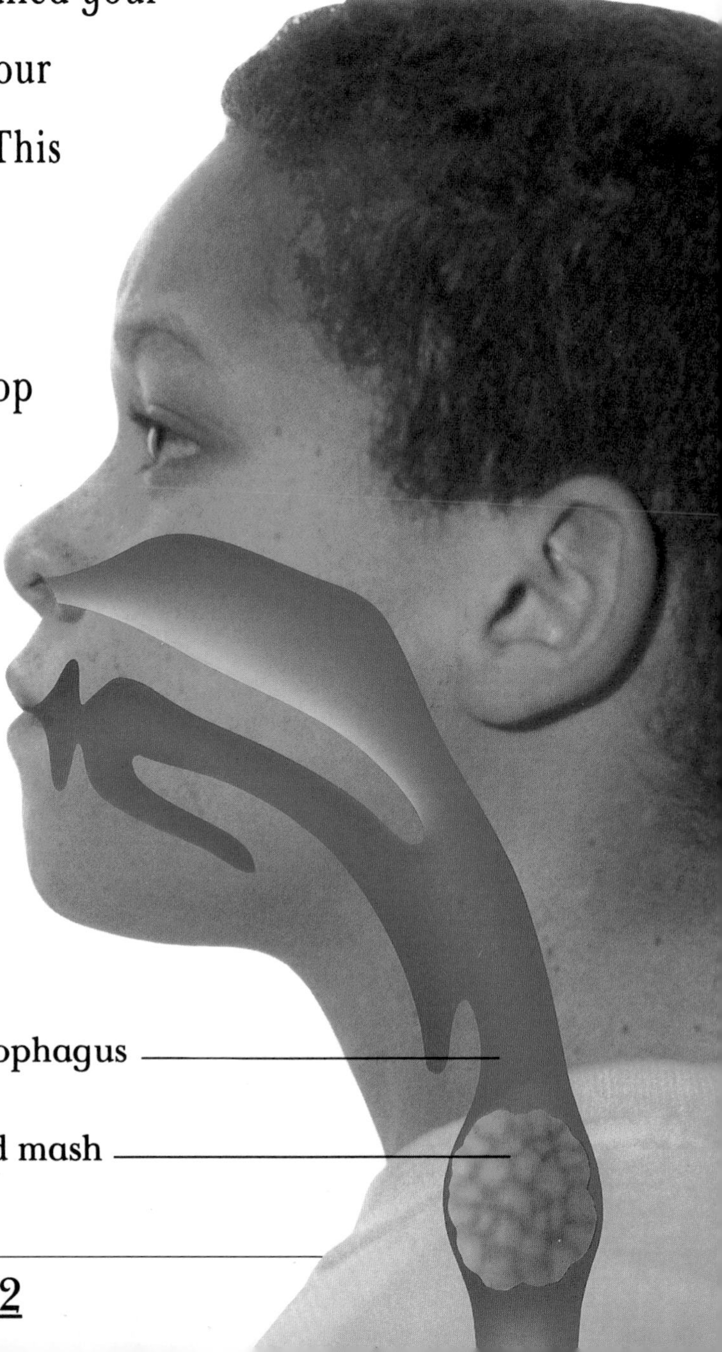

Oesophagus —————————

Food mash —————————

Your oesophagus is a stretchy tube about 25 centimetres long. Its walls are made of muscles which squeeze food downwards. They do this without you thinking about it. To see how they work, put a tennis ball down a long sock. Like the muscles in your oesophagus, you have to squeeze your hands hard together just behind the ball to move it along.

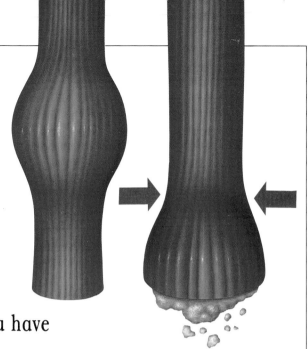

Muscles squeeze behind the food to push it down.

Because food is squeezed along your oesophagus, and does not simply fall down it, it is possible to eat in almost any position – even standing on your head! This means that astronauts can enjoy a meal even when floating around their cabin! (But remember it is safest to eat when you are upright.)

Into your stomach

At the bottom of your oesophagus, the mash passes into your stomach. This is a stretchy bag shaped like a boxing glove. It lies just below your ribs. Food stays here for two to three hours.

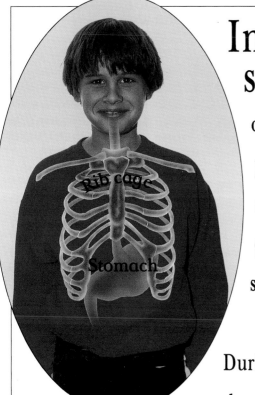

Rib cage

Stomach

During this time, your stomach churns the mash with gastric juices from your stomach wall. These juices kill any germs in the mash and help to break the food down into smaller parts. When the mash has turned into a kind of thick soup, it is ready to leave your stomach.

Gate of muscle

Soup food

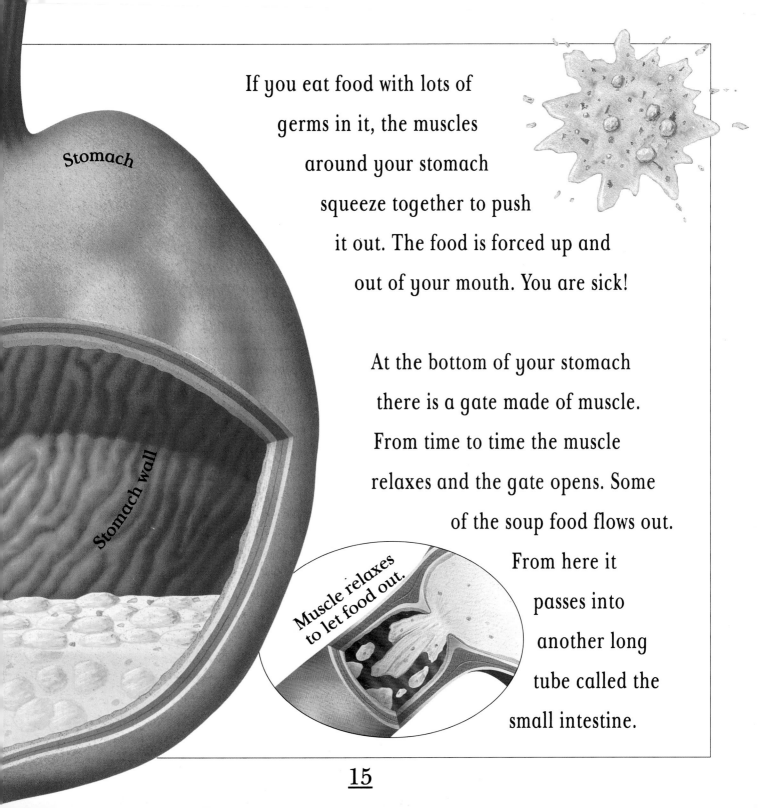

If you eat food with lots of germs in it, the muscles around your stomach squeeze together to push it out. The food is forced up and out of your mouth. You are sick!

Stomach

Stomach wall

At the bottom of your stomach there is a gate made of muscle. From time to time the muscle relaxes and the gate opens. Some of the soup food flows out. From here it passes into another long tube called the small intestine.

Muscle relaxes to let food out.

Your small intestine

Your small intestine is about seven metres long. That's as long as five seven year-olds laid head to toe! It can take up to ten hours for the soup food to travel from one end to the other.

In the first part of the small intestine the soup food is mixed with juices from your pancreas and bile from your liver which helps to break it down even further.

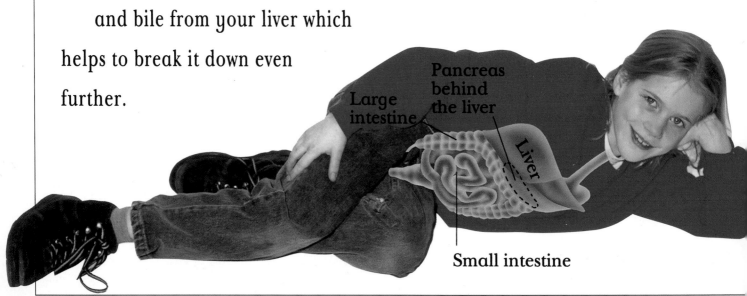

Large intestine

Pancreas behind the liver

Liver

Small intestine

It is then squeezed on through your intestine becoming more and more watery as it goes.

As the almost liquid food reaches the end of your small intestine, nutrients pass through its walls into your blood. The walls are lined with thousands of tiny fingers, called villi, to help digest the nutrients more quickly.

Your blood carries most of the nutrients to your liver. Undigested food travels on to your large intestine.

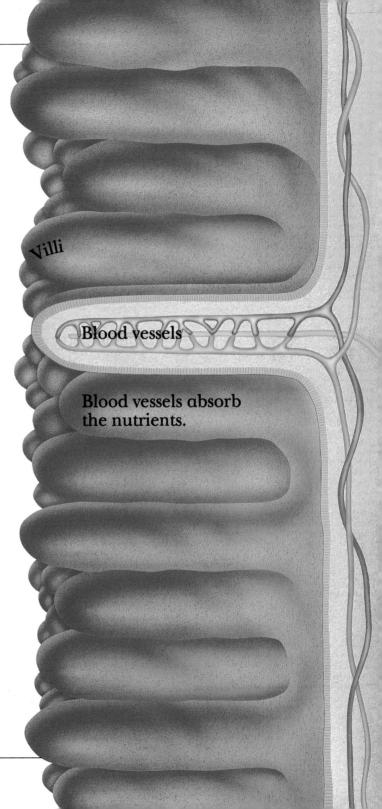

Villi

Blood vessels

Blood vessels absorb the nutrients.

Your liver

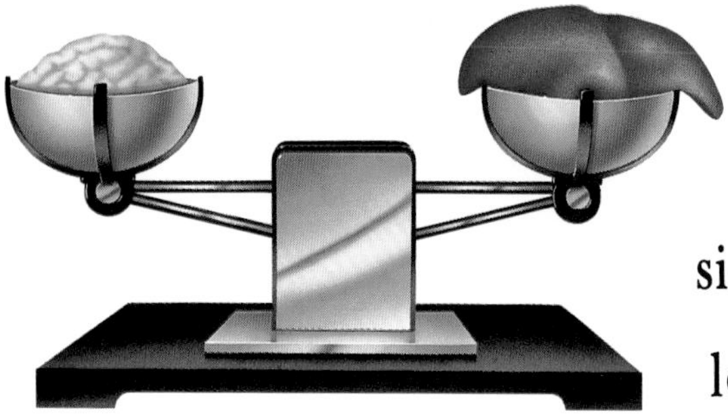

Your liver lies mostly on your right side, protected by your lower ribs. It weighs between one and two kilogrammes. That's about the same weight as your brain.

Before any food can be used by your body, it has to be cleaned and prepared by your liver. Your liver sieves through the nutrients and blood to take out any leftover waste. It turns some of the waste into bile which travels through the bile ducts and out of the liver.

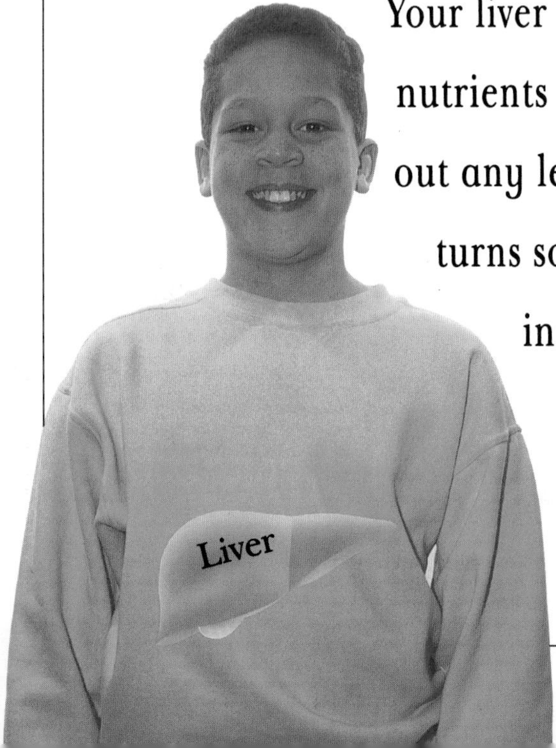

Liver

Liver

Gall bladder

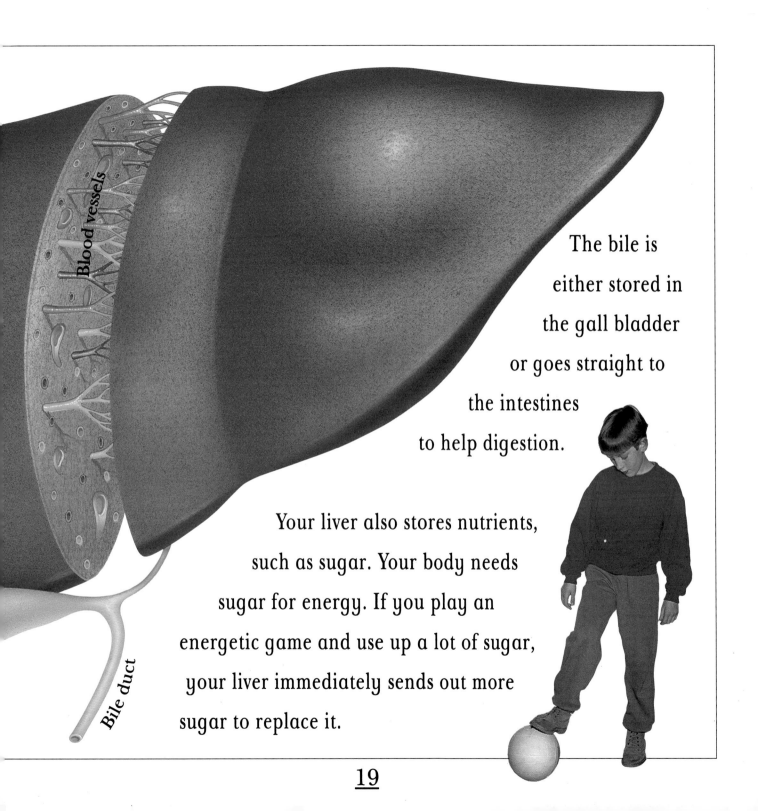

Blood vessels

Bile duct

The bile is either stored in the gall bladder or goes straight to the intestines to help digestion.

Your liver also stores nutrients, such as sugar. Your body needs sugar for energy. If you play an energetic game and use up a lot of sugar, your liver immediately sends out more sugar to replace it.

Your large intestine

Your large intestine carries undigested food and water from your small intestine up, across and down to your rectum.

Your large intestine is wider than your small intestine, but only half as long. It takes up to 24 hours for its contents to complete the journey from beginning to end.

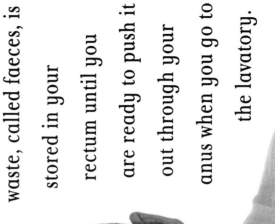

As food and water travel along, a lot of water is sucked through the wall of your large intestine into your blood. Then only waste food is left. Slowly it gets harder. By the time it reaches your rectum, it is quite solid. This solid waste, called faeces, is stored in your rectum until you are ready to push it out through your anus when you go to the lavatory.

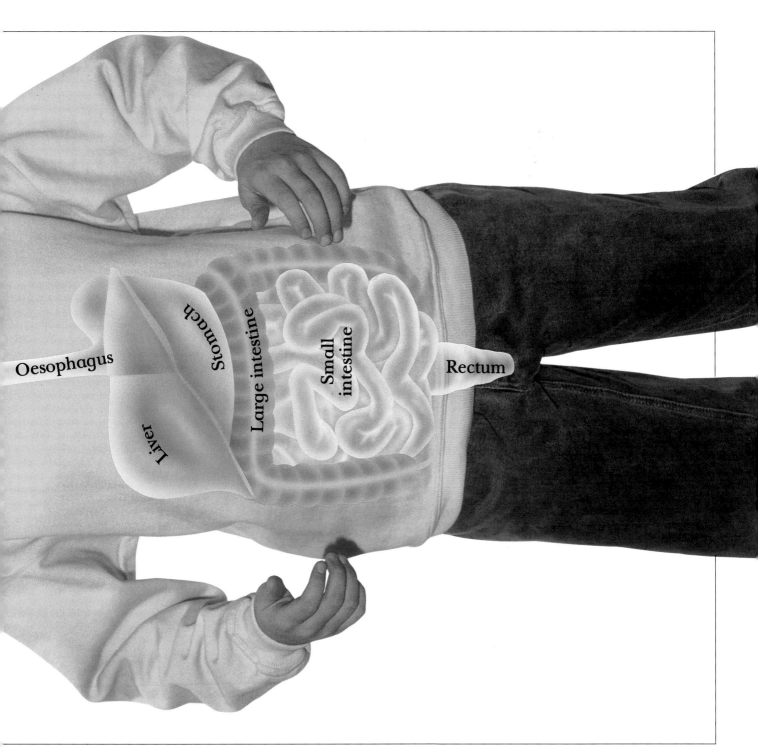

Oesophagus

Liver

Stomach

Large intestine

Small intestine

Rectum

Energy

Most of the food you eat is turned into energy. Some people need more energy – and more food – than others. Babies and young children need less food than grown-ups. As you grow into your teens you need more.

By the time you reach your mid-teens, you will probably eat as much as your parents. Tall, well-built people need more food than shorter, thinner people. Men usually need more than women. If you eat more food than you need it is stored as fat inside your body.

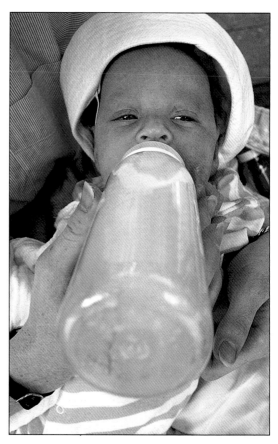

You use energy all the time. Even when you are asleep, your body is using energy to keep warm and make your heart beat. The more active you are, the more energy you use. Which of the activities shown in these pictures do you think uses up most energy? Which uses the least? Put them in order. The answers are at the bottom of the page. Look in a mirror to see if you are right.

Swimming uses the most energy followed by cycling. Watching television uses the least.

Swimming

Watching television

Cycling

Healthy eating

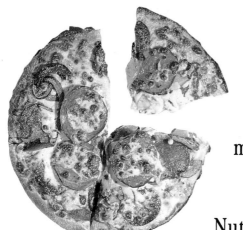

Nutrients are found in food. There are five main types; proteins, carbohydrates, fats, vitamins and mineral salts.

Nutrients are absorbed from the food you eat and used by your body. To stay healthy you should eat the right amount of each type of nutrient every day. Each has one or more special jobs to do in your body.

Proteins help you to grow strong and healthy. The body cannot store them so it is important to eat some food containing proteins every day. They are found in eggs, milk, cheese, fish, meat, beans and nuts.

Bread

Potatoes

Nuts

Meat

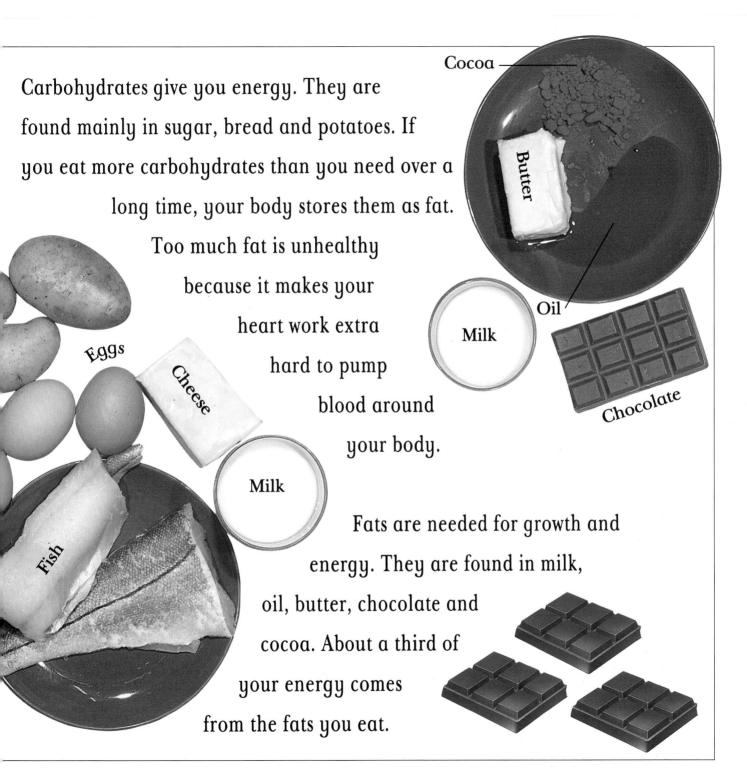

Carbohydrates give you energy. They are found mainly in sugar, bread and potatoes. If you eat more carbohydrates than you need over a long time, your body stores them as fat. Too much fat is unhealthy because it makes your heart work extra hard to pump blood around your body.

Cocoa

Butter

Oil

Milk

Chocolate

Eggs

Cheese

Milk

Fish

Fats are needed for growth and energy. They are found in milk, oil, butter, chocolate and cocoa. About a third of your energy comes from the fats you eat.

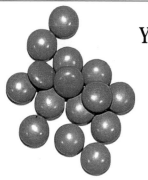

You need small amounts of about 15 vitamins to keep your body working well. Most vitamins are found in several different foods. Vitamin C is present only in fresh fruit and vegetables – especially oranges. Vitamin C is important for healthy skin and bones. It also helps wounds to heal.

Mineral salts are needed only in small amounts. Calcium, in milk and cheese, helps to build healthy bones. Iodine, in fish, is important for growth.

Water

You should drink plenty of water every day. You lose up to two and a quarter litres of water each day when you breathe out, sweat and go to the lavatory. You replace the water by eating as well as drinking. Half of all food is made up of water.

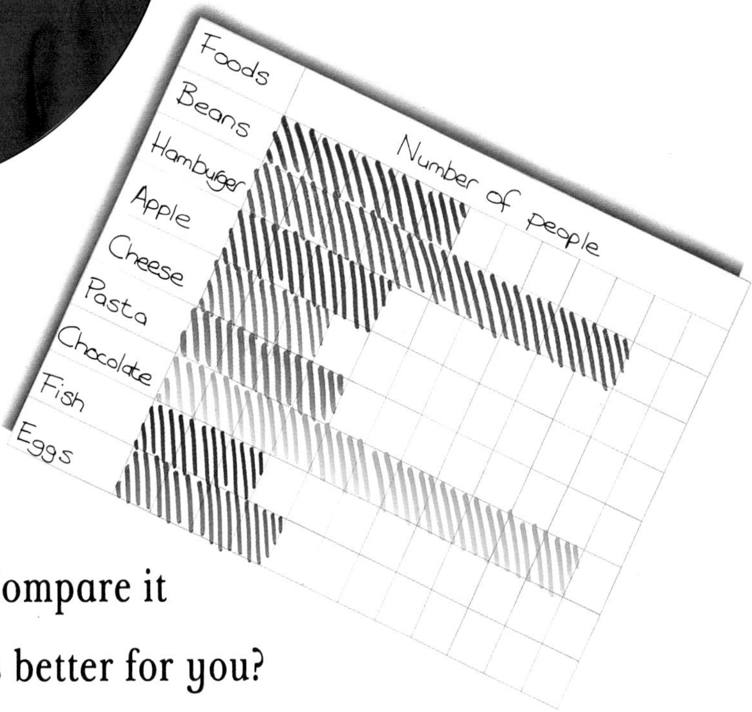

Ask your friends what they like to eat. Make a chart to show everyone's favourite food. Which food do people like the best? Now plan a healthy lunch. Compare it with your favourite meal. Which is better for you?

Foods

Beans

Hamburger

Apple

Cheese

Pasta

Chocolate

Fish

Eggs

Number of people

Did you know?

... that by the age of 70 you will have eaten more than 30,000 kilogrammes of food? That's the same as six elephants or two blue whales.

... that although you could live for up to three weeks without food, you would die in just three days without water?

... that your body has as much calcium as 340 sticks of chalk?

... that nearly three-quarters of your body is made up of water?

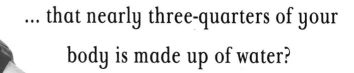

... that the human stomach can hold up to one and a half litres of food and water?

Compare this with a large dog – almost three litres; a pig – between six and nine litres; a horse – between ten and 20 litres; a cow – about 150 litres.

... that every day you produce about one and three-quarter litres of saliva?

Glossary

Bile — fluid from the liver that helps with digestion

Gastric juices — stomach fluids that help you digest food

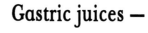

Digestion — the breakdown of food into smaller and smaller pieces, separating it into nutrients and waste matter

Nutrients — the goodness in food

Oesophagus — the tube that takes food from your mouth to your stomach

Epiglottis — a flap over your windpipe that keeps food out of it when you swallow

Saliva — the fluid in your mouth which makes food soft and moist and easier to swallow and digest

Index

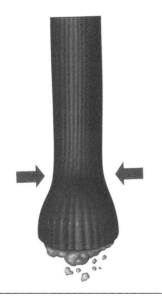

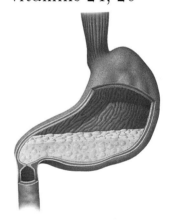

Interested in getting more information about eating and your body?

Check out one of these websites:

www.student.city.ac.uk/~rc313/lev1eats.html

www.kidshealth.org